CRUISING IN STYLE

teNeues

CRUISING IN STYLE

teNeues

Contents

If a little dreaming is dangerous, the cure for it is not to dream less but to dream more, to dream all the time. —*Marcel Proust*

Introduction

MSC Cruises has consistently innovated the design, concepts and services of the luxury cruise holiday since it was founded in 1995, inspired by a typically uncompromising Italian passion for the finer things in life. Sweeping away the past, the strikingly imaginative designs of *MSC Cruises's* purpose-built fleet are unique in their combination of creative originality, the finest materials and detailed attention to real comfort, while its highly-trained, prevalently Italian staff have set new standards in friendly, attentive service.

MSC Cruises has built the most modern cruise fleet in the world, which will comprise twelve ships in three size classes by 2012, all offering superlative standards of variety, comfort and service as they cruise between 200 select destinations across the Mediterranean, Northern Europe, Atlantic Ocean, the Caribbean, the Americas, Indian Ocean, and South Africa.

The new *MSC Fantasia* has inevitably attracted attention with its sheer grandeur. Taller than the Eiffel Tower and one third of a kilometre long, *MSC Fantasia* is like a floating city with an astonishing variety of luxury amenities on board, including a whole array of swimming pools and sports facilities, an exclusive MSC Aurea SPA wellness and spa treatment centre, five varied restaurants, a theatre seating more than 1,600, a casino, discotheque, 18 themed bars, a virtual reality games area with a Formula 1 simulator and a 4-D cinema. The carpets in its public areas extend over 17,000 square metres and the liner features 8,000 square metres of prime marble. Yet despite its size, *MSC Fantasia* respects the environment as it travels, incorporating advanced energy saving, water treatment and hull paint technologies that have won it the prestigious 6 Golden Pearls certification from Bureau Veritas.

But what you are about to discover in these pages is much more than facts and figures. It is a whole world bearing testimony to the vision and teamwork of the people in the *MSC Cruises* family. Because the company *MSC Cruises* operates as a family, led by a passionately dedicated private-owner family at its helm, all are personally and passionately involved in creating cruises that make dreams come true.

You will see all this on every page of this book, although it is perhaps best expressed in the company's latest, entirely innovative luxury concept, MSC Yacht Club – an exclusive ship-within-a-ship of private suites in a luxurious complex with its own concierge, butler service, and sports, leisure and dining amenities. It's a service that offers the best of both worlds: the privacy of a private yacht combined with full and privileged access to the extraordinary variety of superior facilities provided on board *MSC Fantasia*.

This is the world you are about to explore. A world that has itself become a holiday destination no less than the beautiful places visited on each cruise. A world that encapsulates the best in Italian design, with every public area a breathtaking creation of the internationally-renowned De Jorio Design Studio. You will find it a feast for the eyes, from the central Piazza San Giorgio shopping district, a masterpiece in historic Genoese style with stone loggia and original frescoes by Sandro Cubeddu, to the surreal Liquid Disco that projects over the pools and fountains of the Acquapark, and the shimmering Swarovski crystal staircases that spiral up through the ship's receptions. Each picture conveys the passion, creativity and personal touches that *MSC Cruises* brings to making every cruise on every one of its state-of-the-art ships an unforgettable experience.

As you become acquainted with that experience you will not be surprised to learn that *MSC Cruises* has been selected to host the meeting of G8 leaders in July 2009. They will, of course, receive a warm welcome, the same warm welcome we extend to all our passengers.

Welcome to the world of *MSC Cruises*.

Pierfrancesco Vago – *MSC Cruises*' CEO

Introduzione

Sin dalla sua fondazione, nel 1995, *MSC Crociere* ha scelto di percorrere la strada dell'innovazione sia per quanto riguarda il design e le tecnologie adottate, sia per i servizi offerti a bordo, sempre all'insegna dell'Italian Style. La flotta *MSC Crociere* è stata progettata e realizzata con l'obiettivo di innalzare gli standard del settore e creare una combinazione unica di eleganza, materiali preziosi e grande attenzione al confort. I membri dell'equipaggio, in prevalenza italiani, vantano un'esperienza e una cortesia senza paragoni.

La flotta *MSC Crociere* – attualmente la più moderna al mondo – sarà composta nel 2012 da dodici navi di tre classi di grandezza diverse, tutte caratterizzate da un mix perfetto di alta tecnologia, confort e servizi esclusivi, con piu' di duecento destinazioni fra Mediterraneo, Nord Europa, Oceano Atlantico, Carabi, Oceano Indiano e Sudafrica.

Data la sua imponenza, la nuova *MSC Fantasia* non poteva di certo passare inosservata. Più alta della torre Eiffel e lunga quasi trecento metri, questa nave è una vera e propria città galleggiante, con una dotazione incredibilmente ricca di servizi e strutture, fra cui numerose piscine, palestre, aree fitness, l'esclusivo centro benessere MSC Aurea SPA con i suoi trattamenti termali, cinque diversi ristoranti, un teatro da oltre 1.600 posti, un casinò, una discoteca, 18 bar a tema e un'area di svago dedicata alla realtà virtuale con un simulatore di Formula 1 e un cinema 4D. Gli spazi pubblici sono coperti da oltre 17.000 metri quadrati di moquette e da 8.000 metri quadrati di marmo pregiato. Nonostante la grandezza, *MSC Fantasia* sa rispettare l'ambiente grazie alle tecnologie avanzate per il risparmio energetico e il trattamento delle acque e alla speciale verniciatura dello scafo; tutte queste caratteristiche le sono valse la prestigiosa certificazione "6 Golden Pearls" del Bureau Veritas.

In queste pagine tuttavia troverete molto di più di qualche dato o informazione utile: scoprirete un intero universo che riflette lo spirito, la visione e l'impegno comune di tutti i membri di questa compagnia. A cominciare dalla famiglia che la guida con impegno e passione. Tutti con unico obiettivo: trasformare in realtà i sogni di ogni crocierista.

L'eccellenza che *MSC Crociere* dedica a tutti i suoi ospiti traspare da ogni pagina, ma trova la sua espressione più alta nell'ultima novità introdotta a bordo: MSC Yacht Club, un'area esclusiva con suite e servizi di altissimo livello, quali conciergerie, maggiordomo, accesso privato alla MSC Aurea SPA, cucina esclusiva e raffinata, zone per il relax e il tempo libero. Quest'area VIP coniuga la riservatezza di uno yacht privato con l'accesso privilegiato all'incredibile varietà di strutture e servizi presenti a bordo di *MSC Fantasia*.

Ecco il mondo che siete in procinto di esplorare. Un mondo che è già di per sé meta di vacanza al pari delle splendide destinazioni che visiterete. Un mondo che racchiude il meglio del design italiano, dove ogni spazio è una spettacolare creazione del famoso studio De Jorio Design International. Una vera festa per gli occhi. Impossibile non ammirare la straordinaria Piazza San Giorgio, situata al centro della nave, con i suoi negozi e l'atmosfera che ricorda quella delle celebri piazzette di Capri e Portofino, con loggia in pietra e affreschi originali di Sandro Cubeddu. Altrettanta ammirazione suscitano la surreale Liquid Disco, affacciata sulle piscine e le fontane dell'Acquapark, e la scintillante scalinata a spirale realizzata interamente in cristallo Swarovski. Ogni angolo riflette la passione, la creatività e il tocco personale di *MSC Crociere* che rendono la permanenza a bordo un'esperienza indimenticabile.

Adesso che avete scoperto le bellezze di una crociera *MSC*, non sarete sorpresi di apprendere che il G8 di luglio 2009 sarà ospitato proprio a bordo di una nave *MSC*. I leader mondiali saranno accolti con lo stesso caloroso benvenuto che *MSC Crociere* offre a tutti i suoi clienti.

Benvenuti nel mondo di *MSC Crociere*.

Einleitung

Seit seiner Gründung 1995 gelingt es *MSC Kreuzfahrten* immer wieder Design, Konzept und Service ihrer Luxuskreuzfahrten neu zu erfinden. Dabei sind die Schiffsdesigner inspiriert von einer kompromisslosen italienischen Passion für die schönen Dinge des Lebens. Die innovativen Entwürfe der neuen Schiffstypen von *MSC Kreuzfahrten* bestechen durch ihre einzigartige Kombination aus kreativer Originalität, hochwertigen Materialien und der Fokussierung auf größten Komfort. Die hochqualifizierten, vorwiegend italienischen Angestellten setzen zudem durch ihren freundlichen, aufmerksamen Service neue Maßstäbe.

MSC Kreuzfahrten besitzt die modernste Kreuzfahrtflotte der Welt, die 2012 aus zwölf Schiffen – eingeteilt in drei Größenklassen – bestehen wird. Alle bieten die höchsten Standards in puncto Vielfalt, Komfort und Service auf ihren Fahrten zu über 200 Zielorten im Mittelmeer, Nordeuropa, im Atlantik, der Karibik, Nord- und Südamerika, im Indischen Ozean und Südafrika.

Die Pracht der neuen *MSC Fantasia* hat großes Aufsehen erregt. Höher als der Eiffelturm und mit mehr als 300 Metern Länge, wirkt *MSC Fantasia* wie eine schwimmende Stadt. An Bord bietet das Schiff eine unglaubliche Vielfalt an luxuriösen Annehmlichkeiten, wie z. B. eine ganze Reihe von Swimmingpools und Sportmöglichkeiten, ein exklusives MSC Aurea SPA Wellness-Center, fünf verschiedene Restaurants, ein Theater mit mehr als 1.600 Sitzplätzen, ein Kasino, eine Diskothek, 18 Themenbars, ein Virtual-Reality-Spieleraum mit einem Formel 1-Simulator und ein 4D-Kino. Der Teppichboden in den öffentlichen Bereichen allein erstreckt sich über eine Fläche von 17.000 Quadratmetern, während auf dem Schiff mehr als 8.000 Quadratmeter bester Marmor verwendet wurden. Trotz ihrer Größe schont *MSC Fantasia* auf ihren Reisen die Umwelt, indem sie mit neuesten Energie und Wasser sparenden Systemen ausgestattet und ihr Rumpf mit einer Farbe gestrichen wurde, die das Zertifikat „6 Golden Pearls" des Bureau Veritas gewann.

Doch Sie werden in diesem Buch mehr als bloße Fakten und Zahlen entdecken. Eine Welt, in der sich die Visionen und die Teamarbeit der Mitarbeiter der *MSC Kreuzfahrten*-Familie widerspiegeln. Denn das Unternehmen funktioniert wie eine Familie und ist auch im Besitz einer passionierten Familie, deren Mitglieder voller Leidenschaft daran teilhaben, Kreuzfahrten anzubieten, die Urlaubsträume wahr werden lassen.

Diese Begeisterung zeigt sich wohl am besten im neuesten originellen Luxuskonzept der Firma, dem MSC Yacht Club. Es handelt sich hierbei um ein exklusives „Schiff-im-Schiff" mit privaten Suiten, eigenem Concierge, Butlerservice sowie Sport-, Freizeit- und Gastronomieangeboten. Im MSC Yacht Club finden Sie einen Service, der Ihnen die Privatsphäre einer privaten Yacht sowie den privilegierten Zugang zu den außergewöhnlichen Einrichtungen an Bord der *MSC Fantasia* bietet.

Tauchen Sie ein in diese Welt, die bereits ein ebenso begehrtes Urlaubsziel ist wie die herrlichen Orte, die man auf jeder Kreuzfahrt besucht. Eine Welt, die von dem international anerkannten italienischen Design-Studio De Jorio im schönsten italienischen Design konzipiert wurde. Ein Fest für die Sinne, vom zentralen Piazza San Giorgio im historischen Genueser Stil mit Steinloggia und Originalfresken von Sandro Cubeddu bis hin zur surreal wirkenden Liquid Disco, die sich oberhalb der Pools und Brunnen des Acquaparks befindet sowie den mit funkelnden Swarovski-Kristallen bedeckten Treppen, die von der Schiffsrezeption emporsteigen. Jedes Bild vermittelt die Leidenschaft, Kreativität und persönliche Handschrift, durch die eine *MSC Kreuzfahrten*-Reise auf einem der hochmodernen Schiffe zu einem einzigartigen Erlebnis wird.

Wenn Sie diese Welt erlebt haben, werden Sie nicht mehr überrascht sein, dass *MSC Kreuzfahrten* dazu auserwählt wurde, das Treffen der G8-Partner im Juli 2009 auszurichten. Die Gäste werden natürlich herzlich willkommen geheißen, ebenso herzlich wie wir all unsere Gäste an Bord begrüßen.

Willkommen in der Welt von *MSC Kreuzfahrten*.

Introduction

Depuis sa création en 1995, *MSC Croisières*, animée par cette passion du raffinement propre à l'esprit italien, renouvelle le concept de croisière de luxe, notamment en termes de services et d'activités proposés à bord. Tournant résolument la page du passé, les espaces intérieurs des paquebots construits par *MSC Croisières* séduisent par leur façon de combiner originalité des décors, qualité des matériaux et attention portée au confort. Son personnel majoritairement italien veille tout particulièrement à ce dernier aspect en assurant un service irréprochable, aussi amical qu'attentif.

MSC Croisières a constitué la flotte de paquebots de croisière la plus moderne du monde. Elle compter douze navires de trois dimensions différentes d'ici 2012, tous offrant une qualité inégalée en termes d'activités, de confort et de services sur les 200 destinations privilégiées en Méditerranée, en Europe du Nord, dans l'océan Atlantique, aux Caraïbes, aux Amériques, dans l'océan Indien et en Afrique du Sud.

Le *MSC Fantasia*, dernier-né de la flotte, a dernièrement attiré le feu des projecteurs, ne serait-ce que par ses proportions. Plus haut que la tour Eiffel et dépassant les trois cents mètres de long, le *MSC Fantasia* est une véritable ville flottante qui rassemble à son bord une incroyable variété de distractions et d'activités, avec ses piscines de tous formats, ses équipements de sport, son centre de bien-être MSC Aurea SPA, ses cinq restaurants, sa salle de spectacle de plus de 1 600 places, son casino, sa discothèque, ses 18 bars à thème ou encore ses espaces de réalité virtuelle (simulateur de Formule 1, cinéma 4D). Dans les espaces publics, la moquette couvre une surface de plus de 17 000 mètres carrés, et le paquebot compte en tout plus de 8 000 mètres carrés de marbre de première qualité. Malgré sa taille, le *MSC Fantasia* respecte l'environnement. Ses équipements d'avant-garde en matière d'économie d'énergie et de retraitement des eaux usées, ainsi que le type de revêtement employé pour la coque lui ont valu la prestigieuse certification « 6 Golden Pearls » attribuée par le Bureau Veritas.

Mais l'on découvrira à travers ces pages bien plus que des données et des statistiques. C'est tout un univers qui s'ouvre ici au lecteur, un univers qui témoigne à chaque instant des valeurs et du travail d'équipe tel que les conçoit le personnel de *MSC Croisières*. Entreprise familiale fondée sur la passion de la croisière, *MSC Croisières* fonctionne avant tout comme une grande famille dont les membres sont mus par une seule et même aspiration : faire d'une croisière un moment magique où tous les rêves deviennent réalité. Ainsi la magie sera présente à chaque page de cet album, particulièrement à celles consacrées à notre grande nouveauté : le MSC Yacht Club. Cet ensemble de suites situées dans un espace privatif et doté de services et d'équipements exclusifs – conciergerie, majordome, sports, loisirs, restauration – offre au passager le fin du fin en matière d'hébergement de luxe. Dans ce cadre privilégié, il bénéficie de l'intimité d'un yacht privé tout en ayant accès à l'exceptionnelle diversité d'infrastructures mis à sa disposition à bord du *MSC Fantasia*.

Tel est l'univers que vous vous apprêtez à découvrir. Un univers devenu aujourd'hui une destination de vacances à part entière, à l'instar des escales idylliques qui ponctuent chaque croisière. Un univers synonyme d'avant-garde en matière de design italien, où le célèbre studio De Jorio a transformé le moindre espace public en une création d'exception. Aussi bien la Piazza San Georgio, véritable chef-d'œuvre d'architecture classique génoise avec sa loggia en pierre et ses fresques originales de la main de Sandro Cubeddu, que la Liquid Disco, discothèque surréelle qui surplombe les plans d'eau et fontaines de l'Acquapark ou bien encore les gracieux escaliers en cristal Swarovski qui vous accueillent, scintillants, à la réception du navire – tout à bord vous ravira la vue et l'esprit. Chacune des photographies ici rassemblées exprime la passion, la créativité et la singularité apportée par *MSC Croisières* pour faire de toute croisière à bord de ses paquebots d'exception une expérience inoubliable.

Une fois familiarisés avec cette expérience, vous ne serez pas surpris d'apprendre que *MSC Croisières* a été sélectionnée pour accueillir le sommet des pays du G8 qui doit se tenir en juillet 2009. Ces hôtes d'exception recevront bien sûr un accueil chaleureux, celui-là même que nous réservons à tous nos passagers.

Bienvenue dans l'univers de *MSC Croisières*.

Sophia Loren – godmother of the fleet

Introducción

Desde su fundación en 1995, la compañía *MSC Cruceros* ha seguido fiel al constante espíritu innovador de sus diseños, conceptos y servicios en lo que a cruceros de lujo se refiere, inspirado en la tan típica pasión italiana por las cosas buenas de la vida. Dejando atrás el pasado, los extraordinarios e imaginativos diseños de la flota *MSC Cruceros* son únicos gracias a su combinación de original creatividad, los más finos materiales y una esmerada atención al verdadero confort. Asimismo, el personal altamente especializado y en su mayoría de nacionalidad italiana supera todos los estándares de calidad en servicio amable y atento.

La compañía *MSC Cruceros* ha construido la flota de cruceros más moderna del mundo, que en el año 2012 estará formada por doce barcos de tres categorías y dimensiones diferentes, todos ellos con superlativos estándares en la variedad de ofertas, confort y servicios de sus cruceros por 200 selectos destinos a través de aguas del Mediterráneo, del Norte de Europa, del océano Atlántico, del Caribe, de las Américas, del océano Índico y de Sudáfrica.

El nuevo *MSC Fantasia* ha atraído la atención inevitablemente con su impresionante tamaño. Más alto que la torre Eiffel y con más de 300 metros de eslora, el *MSC Fantasia* es una ciudad flotante con una impresionante variedad de comodidades de lujo a bordo, entre las que se incluyen un impresionante conjunto de piscinas e instalaciones deportivas, un centro de tratamiento wellness MSC Aurea SPA, cinco restaurante variados, un teatro con un aforo de más de 1.600 butacas, una discoteca, 18 bares temáticos, un área de juegos de realidad virtual con un simulador de Formula 1 y un cine 4D. Este barco dispone de más de 17.000 metros cuadrados de zonas públicas alfombradas y 8.000 metros cuadrados de suelos de fino mármol. A pesar de sus dimensiones, el *MSC Fantasia* es muy respetuoso con el medio ambiente durante sus travesías ya que incorpora avanzados sistemas de ahorro de energía, depuración de aguas y un pintura de revestimiento especial para el casco que le han valido la prestigiosa certificación "6 Golden Pearls" de la institución Bureau Veritas.

Pero lo que vas a descubrir en estas páginas es mucho más que un conjunto de hechos y cifras, es todo un mundo que da testimonio de la visión y el trabajo en equipo de los miembros de la familia *MSC Cruceros*; y es que la compañía trabaja como un verdadero clan, ya que al timón se sienta la familia propietaria de la compañía que pone verdadera pasión en ofrecer travesías que sean un sueño hecho realidad. Podrás descubrir todo esto en las páginas del libro, aunque sin duda donde mejor se refleja es en el último y completamente innovador concepto de lujo, el MSC Yacht Club: un exclusivo barco dentro del barco, con suites privadas en un complejo de alto standing, recepcionista propio, servicio de mayordomo e instalaciones particulares de deporte, ocio y gastronomía. Este servicio ofrece lo mejor de dos mundos: la intimidad de un yate privado combinada con el completo y privilegiado acceso a la enorme variedad de extraordinarias instalaciones a bordo de *MSC Fantasia*.

Este es el mundo que podrás explorar; un universo que constituye por sí mismo un maravilloso destino de vacaciones tan placentero como los lugares llenos de paz que se visitan en cada travesía; un mundo que encapsula lo mejor del diseño italiano y ofrece en cada una de sus estancias públicas una impresionante creación del internacionalmente renombrado De Jorio Design Studio. El barco será una fiesta para sus sentidos, desde la zona central de compras de la Piazza San Giorgio –una joya concebida en el estilo histórico genovés con una arcada de piedra y frescos originales realizados por Sandro Cubeddu– a la surrealista Liquid Disco, que se asoma a las piscinas y surtidores del Acquapark, y la centelleante escalera de cristal de Swarovski que asciende en espiral por las recepciones del barco. Cada rincón refleja la pasión, la creatividad y el toque personal que *MSC Cruceros* desea ofrecer para hacer que las travesías en todos y cada uno de sus modernísimos barcos resulten una experiencia inolvidable.

Así, una vez familiarizado con tal experiencia no te sorprenderás al saber que *MSC Cruceros* ha sido elegido como el lugar para el encuentro de los líderes del G8 en julio de 2009. Por supuesto, los participantes serán recibidos cálidamente, con la misma hospitalidad que reservamos a todos y a cada uno de nuestros pasajeros.

Bienvenidos al mundo de *MSC Cruceros*.

Page 11: *MSC Daniela*, the largest container ship of the *Mediterranean Shipping Company* (14.000 TEUs)
Page 13: *MSC Crociere's* top priority: the environment, and in particular the sea.

MSC Fantasia

MSC Fantasia launched a new era of luxury in December 2008. Designed for beauty without compromise, its wealth of different lounges, bars, dance, music, and dining venues each boast a distinctive style of their own, set off by sweeping Swarovski crystal staircases and – behind the scenes – the refined opulence of the private MSC Yacht Club with its exclusive butler service. A host of advanced energy-saving, water treatment and waste processing systems combine to create an ecological marvel that glides through the waters with absolutely no impact on the sea, making *MSC Fantasia* both the most beautiful ship in the world and the most ecological too.

Dicembre 2008: *MSC Fantasia* ridefinisce il concetto di lusso. Concepita per offrire un'eleganza senza compromessi, questo gioiello del mare dispone di innovative aree per il divertimento e il tempo libero: bar, discoteche, ristoranti e locali, ognuno con un proprio stile. L'imponente scalinata in cristallo Swarovski e la raffinatezza di MSC Yacht Club – l'esclusiva area VIP con servizio di maggiordomo – sono solo alcune delle meraviglie presenti a bordo. I moderni sistemi di risparmio energetico, trattamento delle acque e smaltimento dei rifiuti consentono a *MSC Fantasia* di solcare gli oceani senza alcun impatto sull'ecosistema marino e la rendono la nave più ecologica del mondo, oltre che la più bella.

Mit *MSC Fantasia* wurde im Dezember 2008 eine neue Ära des Luxus eingeläutet. Hier steht das kompromisslos schöne Design im Vordergrund. Die zahlreichen Lounges, Bars und Restaurants erstrahlen in unverwechselbaren Stilrichtungen, umrahmt von ausladenden Treppen mit Swarovski-Kristallen und – hinter den Kulissen – begleitet von der kultivierten Opulenz des privaten MSC Yacht Clubs mit seinem exklusiven Butlerservice. Durch Energie und Wasser sparende Systeme sowie eine ausgeklügelte Abfallwirtschaft wurde zudem ein ökologisches Juwel geschaffen, das ohne jegliche Belastung für das Meer durch die Wellen gleitet. So ist *MSC Fantasia* nicht nur das schönste, sondern auch das umweltfreundlichste Schiff der Welt.

Avec le *MSC Fantasia*, s'ouvre en décembre 2008 une nouvelle ère du luxe. D'une élégance sans compromis, le paquebot offre une profusion de salons, de bars, de discothèques, de salles de concert et de restaurants : autant de lieux dotés d'un style bien à eux. Cette profusion est rehaussée par de somptueux escaliers en cristal Swarovski et – en coulisse – par l'opulence et le raffinement du MSC Yacht Club, espace privé disposant d'un service de majordome exclusif. Doté de nombreux systèmes ultramodernes permettant de réaliser des économies d'énergie, de retraiter les eaux usées et de recycler les déchets, le *MSC Fantasia*, véritable merveille technologique à même de sillonner les mers sans le moindre impact sur l'environnement, s'affirme comme le paquebot non seulement le plus beau, mais aussi le plus écologique du monde.

Con *MSC Fantasia* en diciembre de 2008 se inauguró una nueva era en lo que al lujo se refiere. Diseñado buscando la belleza sin compromiso, este barco dispone de diversos salones, bares, salas de baile y música, y comedores. Todas las estancias hacen alarde de un estilo distintivo y propio, resaltado por una amplia escalinata de cristal de Swarovski y, entre bastidores, la refinada opulencia del MSC Yacht Club, una sociedad privada con un exclusivo servicio de mayordomo. La combinación de varios sistemas de ahorro de energía, depuración de aguas y procesamiento de basuras crean una maravilla ecológica que se desliza sobre las aguas sin ningún impacto sobre el mar y hacen de *MSC Fantasia* el barco más bonito del mundo y también el más ecológico.

FACTS & FIGURES

Gross Tonnage:	137,936 tons	**Public areas:**	25 lifts (including 1 for Yacht Club),
Length:	333.33 metres		art gallery, 6 restaurants, 22 bars,
Height:	66.8 metres		5 pools, 12 SPA baths, solarium,
Width:	37.92 metres		disco, 4D cinema, Formula 1
Cruising speed:	22.55 knots		simulator, casino and shops
Passenger decks:	13		plus a 1,700-square metre spa
Cabins:	1637, including 43 for passengers with		treatment centre and the exclusive
	disabilities (3.274 passengers on double		MSC Yacht Club with private areas
	basis/maximum capacity: 3.959)		and services
External cabins with balcony: 1.151			

Page 23: Lido Catalano – ZEN Area
Page 24/25: Detail of the funnel

Top left: Lido Catalano – ZEN Area
Bottom left: Il Polo Nord – children area
Right: Lido Catalano – ZEN Area

Main hall and reception with panoramic lifts and transparent piano

Page 30/31: Reception with Swarovski staircase

Bottom left: I Graffiti – Teen disco
Top left and right: Liquid Disco: pink drops and waves everywhere

Manhattan Bar – Jazz bar

Page 36/37: MSC Yacht Club – the concierge desk with Swarovski cristal staircase

Top Sail Lounge in the MSC Yacht Club

Page 40–43: Il Transatlantico – piano bar

Page 44/45: Il Cappuccino – coffee bar

Top left: Red Velvet – staircase uniting both restaurant halls
Bottom left: Red Velvet – intimate alcove
Right: Red Velvet – main restaurant on two decks

Il Cerchio d'Oro – panoramic restaurant

Bottom left: Sports Bar – this motorcycle belonged to the several times World Champion Giacomo Agostini
Right: Sports Bar

Page 52/53: L'Insolito lounge
Page 54/55: Piazza San Giorgio – Italian-style square in Ligurian tradition, paved in stone with a ceiling simulating day and night

L'Étoile – French restaurant à la carte

Page 58/59: El Sombrero – Tex-Mex restaurant with its beautiful Cadillac at the entrance

Zanzibar – cafeteria

Left: Casino delle Palme – detail of the stairway leading to the upper deck
Right: Casino delle Palme

Page 64/65: La Caramella – candy/sweet shop

MSC Yacht Club suite with private balcony

Bottom left: Acqua Park – swimming pools and whirlpool baths and at night, a fountain with light show and music
Right: Lido Catalano – ZEN Area

Il Polo Nord – children area

Bottom left: Turkish bath
MSC Aurea SPA – wellness, relaxation and Balinese massages

Page 74/75: MSC Aurea SPA – relaxation area

Top left: MSC Aurea SPA – fitness centre
Right: MSC Aurea SPA – one of the massage rooms

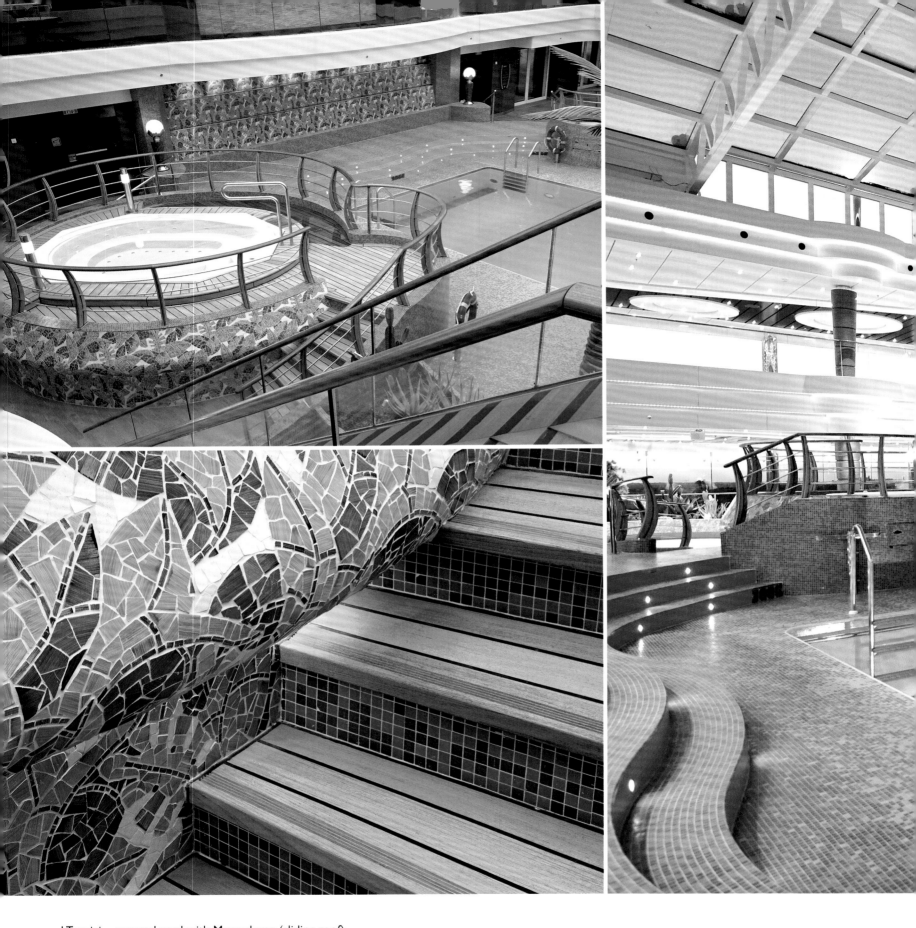

I Tropici – covered pool with Magrodome (sliding roof)

Top left: Engine room
Page 81 left: *MSC Fantasia's* Captain, Giuliano Bossi
Page 81 right: The bridge

MSC Poesia

MSC Poesia, the third ship in the Musica class, continued its predecessors' ceaseless innovation. Launched in April 2008 with ecological engines and green waste management, it was the first cruise ship to adopt Intersleek 900 paint, which keeps the underwater hull clean without using polluting biocides. The result is doubly green, since the sleeker hull glides through the water more easily, improving fuel efficiency and reducing emissions. Enhancing the acclaimed amenities of the Musica class, *MSC Poesia* features a showcase MSC Aurea SPA wellness centre, a sushi bar, two cocktail bars and innovative designer-themed areas – poetry in motion.

MSC Poesia, la terza nave della classe Musica, rispetta la tradizione di continua innovazione che ha caratterizzato le navi precedenti. Varata nell'aprile 2008, dispone di motori a basso impatto ambientale e di un efficiente sistema di smaltimento dei rifiuti. MSC Poesia inoltre è stata la prima nave da crociera ad adottare la vernice Intersleek 900, che mantiene pulita la chiglia sommersa senza l'impiego di biocidi inquinanti. Il risultato è duplice: la superficie della chiglia resta più liscia e pulita e oppone minore resistenza, migliorando l'efficienza dei consumi e riducendo le emissioni. La *MSC Poesia* arricchisce l'offerta di intrattenimento e relax della classe Musica, con il centro benessere MSC Aurea SPA, un sushi bar, due cocktail bar e innovative aree a tema. È davvero poesia in movimento…

MSC Poesia ist das dritte Schiff der Musica-Klasse und setzt die Reihe der Innovationen ihrer Vorgängerinnen fort. Mit ökologischen Motoren und effizienter Abfallwirtschaft ausgestattet, wurde es im April 2008 vom Stapel gelassen. Es war das erste Kreuzfahrtschiff mit Intersleek 900-Farbe, die den Schiffsrumpf unter Wasser sauber hält, ohne verschmutzende Biozide abzugeben. Das Ergebnis ist zweifach ökologisch, da der schlankere Schiffsrumpf auch leichter durch das Wasser gleitet und somit das Schiff weniger Diesel verbraucht und Abgase produziert. Auf *MSC Poesia* wurden die gefeierten Annehmlichkeiten der Musica-Klasse noch verbessert. Hier finden sich ein MSC Aurea SPA Wellness-Center, eine Sushibar, zwei Cocktailbars und innovative Designräumlichkeiten. Poesie in Bewegung …

Troisième paquebot de la classe Musica, le *MSC Poesia* poursuit l'incessante quête d'innovation de ses prédécesseurs. Inauguré en avril 2008 avec des moteurs écologiques et un système de recyclage des déchets, le *MSC Poesia* est le premier navire de croisière à disposer d'un revêtement Intersleek 900, empêchant l'incrustation d'organismes marins sur la partie immergée de la coque et évitant le recours à des produits polluants. Le bénéfice écologique est ici double : la coque, plus lisse, fend plus aisément les flots, ce qui permet de réduire à la fois la consommation de carburant et les émissions de gaz à effet de serre. Outre l'impressionnante gamme de services et d'activités proposée à bord des navires de la classe Musica, le *MSC Poesia* met à la disposition des passagers un centre de soin et de bien-être MSC Aurea SPA, un bar à sushi, deux bars à cocktails ainsi que divers espaces à thèmes des plus originaux. De la poésie en mouvement …

MSC Poesia, tercer navío de la clase Musica, continúa cultivando el carácter innovador de sus predecesores. Inaugurado en abril de 2008, dispone de motores ecológicos y de un sistema de tratamiento de residuos verdes, además de ser el primer barco de crucero tratado con la pintura especial Intersleek 900 que mantiene limpio el caso sumergido sin necesidad de usar biocidas contaminantes. El resultado es doblemente respetuoso con el medio ambiente porque el casco brillante y liso surca con más facilidad las aguas, lo que mejora la eficiencia del consumo de combustible y reduce las emisiones. Como mejora a las aclamadas comodidades de la clase Musica, *MSC Poesia* dispone de un ejemplar centro de bienestar, el MSC Aurea SPA, un restaurante de sushi, dos bares de cócteles e innovadoras áreas de diseños temáticos. Pura poesía en acción …

FACTS & FIGURES

Gross Tonnage:	93,000 tons	**Public areas:**	22.000 square metres, including
Length:	293.8 metres		13 lifts, 7 themed areas, 5 restaurants,
Height:	59.64 metres		15 bars, 3 swimming pools, 4 SPA
Width:	32.2 metres		baths and a 1.160-square metre spa
Cruising speed:	23 knots		treatment centre
Passenger decks:	13		
Cabins:	1.275 (2.550 passengers on a double basis/maximum capacity: 3.013)		

Page 83–85: The Zebra Bar

Page 86/87: Coral Bay pool area

Pigalle lounge bar

Page 90/91: S32 Disco
Page 92/93: *MSC Poesia* sailing through the Venice lagoon

Left: Casino Royal
Right: Poker room

Top left: Entrance of the Carlo Felice Theatre
Right: Carlo Felice Theatre – 1.240 seats

Page 98 left: Engine room
Page 98 right: Engine control room
Page 99 right: Captain Ferdinando Ponti and one of his officers

Outside cabin with balcony

Page 102–105: Kaito – sushi bar and Japanese restaurant

Page 106/107: *MSC Poesia* with its 89.600 tons

Page 108–111: The Galleys (kitchens)

Left: Pool area Coral Bay
Right: Detail of pool area Cayo Levantado

Page 114/115: MSC Aurea SPA – relaxation area with three whirlpools

Right: MSC Aurea SPA – reception

MSC Orchestra

MSC Orchestra, the second ship in the Musica class, was launched in May 2007, making it clear that *MSC Cruises* was not a company to rest on its laurels. Building on the astonishing qualities that won its predecessor international acclaim, the most significant technical advance – featured on every *MSC Cruises* ship to follow – was an innovative system that cuts engine noise by a whole 5 decibels using a system of air nozzles to create a shock-absorbing cushion under the hull. Other firsts included a themed Chocolate Bar complete with chocolate fountain and an authentic Chinese restaurant with 360-degree views across the sea.

Varata nel maggio 2007, *MSC Orchestra*, la seconda nave della classe Musica, testimonia l'impegno costante profuso da *MSC Crociere* nell'offrire crociere di livello sempre più elevato. Partendo dalle eccezionali caratteristiche della nave precedente è stata introdotta un'importante innovazione tecnologica, poi applicata a tutte le navi successive della flotta *MSC Crociere*: un sistema di nuova concezione che consente di ridurre di 5 decibel il rumore dei motori, grazie a un sistema che crea un cuscinetto d'aria sotto lo scafo per assorbire urti e rumori. Fra le altre novità introdotte a bordo: il Chocolate Bar, un bar a tema, con fontana di cioccolato e un vero ristorante cinese con vista a 360 gradi sul mare.

MSC Orchestra, das zweite Schiff der Musica-Klasse, wurde im Mai 2007 vom Stapel gelassen und bewies, dass *MSC Kreuzfahrten* kein Unternehmen ist, das sich auf seinen Lorbeeren ausruht. Die herausragenden Eigenschaften, die schon ihrer Vorgängerin internationalen Ruhm einbrachten, wurden weiterentwickelt. Die bedeutendste technische Neuerung ist ein innovatives System, das den Motorenlärm um 5 Dezibel verringert und nun auf jedem der nachfolgenden *MSC Kreuzfahrten*-Schiffe eingesetzt wird. Es handelt sich um eine Konstruktion aus Luftdüsen, die ein stoßdämpfendes Kissen unter dem Bootskörper bildet. Außerdem finden sich zum ersten Mal eine Chocolate Bar mit Schokoladenbrunnen sowie ein authentisches chinesisches Restaurant mit einem 360°-Panoramablick auf das Meer an Bord.

Deuxième paquebot de la classe Musica, le *MSC Orchestra* est inauguré en mai 2007, affirmant haut et fort que *MSC Croisières* n'est pas de ces compagnies qui se reposent sur leurs lauriers. Mettant à profit les qualités exceptionnelles qui ont valu à son prédécesseur une renommée internationale, le *MSC Orchestra* bénéficie d'une avancée technique remarquable – appliquée depuis à tous les paquebots de *MSC Croisières* – à savoir un système innovant de propulsion d'air permettant de former un coussin antichoc sous la coque et de réduire de cinq décibels le bruit du moteur. Autres points forts du *MSC Orchestra* : son Chocolate Bar avec sa fontaine à chocolat et son authentique restaurant chinois avec vue panoramique sur la mer.

MSC Orchestra es el segundo barco en la clase Musica, cuya botadura en mayo de 2007 dio fé de que la compañía *MSC Cruceros* no se duerme en los laureles. Continuando con la impresionante calidad que le valió a su predecesor prestigio internacional, su avance técnico más significativo, adoptado luego en todos los barcos de la flota de *MSC Cruceros*, fue un innovador sistema que reduce el sonido del motor a 5 decibelios por medio de un dispositivo de toberas de aire comprimido bajo el casco que crea un efecto de insonorización. Entre otras innovaciones destaca el Chocolate Bar –un local temático con una fuente de chocolate–, y un auténtico restaurante chino con una vista de 360 grados sobre el mar.

FACTS & FIGURES

Gross Tonnage:	92,409 tons	**Public areas:**	13 lifts, 5 restaurants, 15 bars, casino,
Length:	293.8 metres		theatre, Internet café, 3 swimming
Height:	59.64 metres		pools, 4 SPA baths, 1.160-square
Width:	32.2 metres		metre spa
Cruising speed:	22.9 knots		
Passenger decks:	13		
Cabins:	1.275 (2.550 passengers on double basis)		

Page 119–121: L'Incontro – reception

Left: Captain Mario Stiffa and one of his officers
Right: Outside decks

The Savannah Bar

Page 128/129: The Purple Bar

Left: Pool area Cala Blanca
Right: Sports area

Shanghai – Chinese restaurant

Villa Borghese restaurant

Page 136–139: Internet café

Library

Page 142: Photo shop
Page 143: Photo gallery

Minigolf

MSC Musica

MSC Cruises and De Jorio caused a sensation with *MSC Musica* in June 2006. A full 50% larger than its illustrious predecessors, the first ship in the Musica class introduced entirely new levels not just of grandeur, but of variety and spectacle, from the swooping staircases of the Cascata reception to a spellbinding three-deck waterfall and the immense vaulted La Scala theatre, constellated with tiny lights. Passenger comfort and style were also revolutionised, with 85% of all accommodation enjoying ocean views and over half boasting private balconies. No wonder so many have sung *MSC Musica's* praises as in a class of its own!

A giugno 2006, quando è stata varata la nuova *MSC Musica*, *MSC Crociere* e lo studio De Jorio Design International hanno rivoluzionato gli standard del settore. *MSC Musica*, infatti, è 50 % più grande delle navi costruite in precedenza – ma anche per la varietà e la bellezza degli spazi, dalla maestosa scalinata della reception La Cascata, alla spettacolare parete d'acqua, fino all'immenso teatro La Scala, con il suo soffitto punteggiato di minuscole luci. Anche il confort di bordo e lo stile di viaggio sono stati rivoluzionati: 85 % delle cabine ha la vista sul mare e oltre la metà è dotata di balcone privato. Non c'è dunque da meravigliarsi che, sin dal primo momento, *MSC Musica* abbia attirato su di sé solo sguardi di ammirazione!

Im Juni 2006 erregten *MSC Kreuzfahrten* und De Jorio mit dem Neubau von *MSC Musica* großes Aufsehen. Ganze 50 % größer als ihre illustren Vorgängerinnen, bot das erste Schiff der Musica-Klasse eine neue Pracht, Vielfalt und spektakuläre Attraktionen – von den geschwungenen Prunktreppen der Cascata-Rezeption bis zu dem atemberaubenden, drei Decks hohen Wasserfall und dem gewaltigen Gewölbe des Theaters La Scala, das von winzigen Lichtern geschmückt ist. Ebenso wurden der Komfort und Stil für die Reisenden revolutioniert. 85 % aller Kabinen bieten einen Blick auf den Ozean, mehr als die Hälfte besitzen zudem private Balkone. Kein Wunder also, dass so viele Gäste *MSC Musica* als Klasse für sich sehen.

MSC Croisières et l'architecte d'intérieur De Jorio font sensation en juin 2006, lors de l'inauguration du *MSC Musica*. Plus vaste de 50 % au moins que ses illustres prédécesseurs, le premier navire de la classe Musica atteint en effet un niveau inégalé non seulement en termes de proportions, mais aussi de diversité et de féérie avec l'impressionnant escalier de la réception Cascata, l'éblouissante cascade sur trois étages, sans oublier l'immense théâtre La Scala à la voûte constellée de lumières. Les passagers bénéficient, eux aussi, d'une petite révolution en termes de confort et de décoration. 85 % des cabines ont en effet vue sur mer et la moitié d'entre elles dispose d'un balcon privé. Il n'est guère étonnant dans ces conditions que tant d'observateurs considèrent le *MSC Musica* comme un paquebot à nul autre pareil.

La compañía *MSC Cruceros* y el estudio de diseño De Jorio causaron sensación en junio de 2006 con *MSC Musica*. Nada más y nada menos que con un 50 % más de capacidad que sus ilustres predecesores, el primer barco de la clase Musica presentaba nuevos cánones no sólo en cuanto a su magnificencia, sino también por la variedad y espectacularidad de sus instalaciones, desde la vertiginosa escalera de la recepción Cascata, con su encantador salto de agua de tres cubiertas de altura, al grandioso y abovedado teatro La Scala y su firmamento cuajado de diminutas luces. Con este barco se revolucionaron también los conceptos de confort y estilo, ya que un 85 % de los camarotes ofrecen vistas al océano y más de la mitad están dotados de balcones privados. ¡No es de extrañar que *MSC Musica* haya sido tan aclamado por su extraordinaria categoría!

FACTS & FIGURES

Gross Tonnage:	92,409 tons	**Public areas:**	13 lifts, 4 restaurants, 15 bars, casino,
Length:	293.8 metres		theatre, Internet café, tennis court,
Height:	59.64 metres		3 swimming pools, 4 SPA baths,
Width:	32.2 metres		1.160-square metre wellness and
Cruising speed:	22 knots		spa treatment centre
Passenger decks:	13		
Cabins:	1.275 (2.550 passengers on a double basis/maximum capacity: 3.013)		

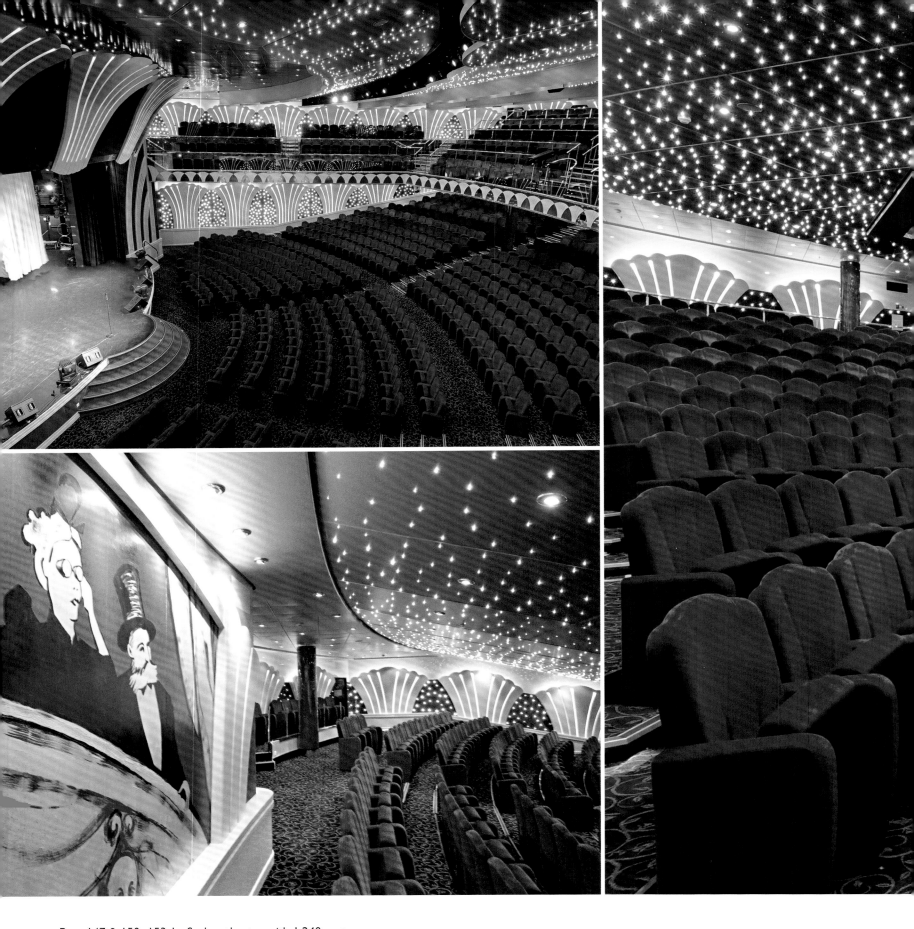

Page 147 & 150–153: La Scala – theatre with 1.240 seats.

Le Maxim's restaurant – Mediterranean cuisine

Pool area Copacabana

Page 158/159: Pool area La Spiaggia
Page 160–162: Il Tucano lounge bar

Right: Art deco-style staircase leading from Il Tucano lounge to the Casino Sanremo

Page 164–167: Kaito – sushi bar and Japanese restaurant

Page 168/169: *MSC Musica* in Santorini (Greece)

La Cascata reception

Left: Balinese hot lava stones massage
Right: MSC Aurea SPA – entrance of the sauna

Page 174/175: Relaxation area

Left: Children area Musica Playland
Right: Children indoor playroom

MSC Opera

MSC Opera, the second ship in the Lirica class, was launched in June 2004. Distinguished by the same design virtuosity and variety of leisure and entertainment as its sister ship *MSC Lirica*, it differs in showcasing *MSC Cruises'* uniquely Italian identity. The striking interiors have been ingeniously conceived for both space and privacy, with sweeping contemporary lines that boldly declare their art deco heritage in geometric shapes, polished brass, mirrors and marble floors. Focusing on relaxation no less than recreation, *MSC Opera* boasts a fully-equipped wellness centre with floor-to-ceiling windows matched by cabins that are havens of peace and comfort.

MSC Opera, la seconda nave della classe Lirica, è stata varata nel giugno 2004. Contraddistinta dallo stesso design raffinato che caratterizza la sua gemella *MSC Lirica*, *MSC Opera* è un vero gioiello che porta in alto la bandiera dello stile italiano. Gli splendidi interni sono progettati per coniugare le esigenze di spazio e di privacy, con linee contemporanee che mostrano con orgoglio le loro radici art déco in forme geometriche, lucidi ottoni, specchi e pavimenti in marmo. Su *MSC Opera* l'accento è posto sul relax e sull'intrattenimento: il centro benessere con le sue vetrate panoramiche è perfettamente attrezzato, mentre le accoglienti cabine rappresentano un'oasi di tranquillità e confort.

MSC Opera, das zweite Schiffe der Lirica-Klasse, wurde im Juni 2004 getauft. Genauso elegant und mit einer ebenso großen Auswahl an Unterhaltungs- und Freizeitmöglichkeiten wie ihr Schwesterschiff *MSC Lirica* ausgestattet, unterscheidet es sich lediglich durch die für *MSC Kreuzfahrten* typische, unverwechselbare italienische Lebensart, die überall an Bord spürbar ist. Die eindrucksvollen Interieurs wurden so konzipiert, dass sie gleichermaßen Geräumigkeit wie Intimität in einem zeitgenössischen Design bieten, welches das Art-Déco-Erbe in geometrischen Formen, glänzendem Messing, Spiegeln und Marmorböden kongenial aufnimmt. *MSC Opera* konzentriert sich ganz auf Entspannung und Erholung, was sich u.a. im Wellness-Center mit seinen raumhohen Fenstern und den Kabinen zeigt, allesamt Oasen der Ruhe und des Komforts.

Inauguré en 2004, le *MSC Opera* est le deuxième paquebot de la classe Lirica. S'il réunit les mêmes qualités que son prédécesseur, le *MSC Lirica* – virtuosité de l'architecture intérieure et diversité des activités et divertissements proposés – le *MSC Opera* s'en distingue par son identité exclusivement italienne. Ses superbes espaces intérieurs ont été conçus pour offrir au passager autant d'espace que d'intimité. Lignes contemporaines majestueuses, formes géométriques, cuivres polis, miroirs et sols en marbre : le moindre détail affiche ici son héritage art déco. Honorant à la fois divertissement et relaxation, le *MSC Opera* met à la disposition des passagers un centre de bien-être parfaitement équipé et doté de baies vitrées que l'on retrouve également dans les cabines, véritables havres de paix et de confort.

MSC Opera, el segundo barco de la clase Lirica, fue botado en junio de 2004. Caracterizado por un idéntico virtuosismo en el diseño y la misma variedad de ofertas de ocio y entretenimiento que su gemelo el barco *MSC Lirica*, la única diferencia es la distintiva identidad italiana de *MSC Cruceros*. Sus notables interiores han sido ingeniosamente concebidos para ofrecer al mismo tiempo generosidad espacial e intimidad. Las arrebatadoras y contemporáneas líneas revelan su inspiración en el art-déco con los característicos motivos geométricos, latón pulido, espejos y suelos de mármol. Con un no menor interés por la relajación que por el recreo, el *MSC Opera* dispone de un centro de bienestar de paredes acristaladas completamente equipado y de camarotes que constituyen un paraíso de paz y confort.

FACTS & FIGURES

Gross Tonnage:	59,058 tons	**Public areas:** 9 lifts, 4 restaurants, 12 bars, casino,
Length:	251.25 metres	Internet café, tennis court, 2 swimming
Height:	54 metres	pools, 2 SPA baths, jogging track, gym,
Width:	28.80 metres	solarium, minigolf, theatre, disco, casino
Cruising speed:	21.7 knots	
Passenger decks:	9	
Cabins:	856 (1.712 passengers, on a double basis/maximum capacity: 2.055)	

Page 181: Pool area
Page 182/183: Sotto Vento pub

Left: Pool area
Middle: The Spinnaker – pool bar
Right: Jogging track

MSC Lirica

Launched in Naples in April 2003, *MSC Lirica* was the ship which established *MSC Cruises* as an undisputed innovator in luxury cruising. The ground-breaking design by De Jorio Design International combines a modern architectural vision of *MSC Lirica's* extensive leisure and entertainment facilities with traditional materials and craftsmanship of the finest quality. Striking contrasts result, spanning the classic grand marble staircase, futuristic shimmering glass walls of the Blue Club disco and typically English décor of the Lord Nelson pub. It is this incredible variety of styles and amenities that makes *MSC Lirica* a ship one never tires of exploring.

MSC Lirica, varata a Napoli nell'aprile 2003 è stata la prima ammiraglia di nuova generazione. Il design innovativo, firmato dallo studio De Jorio Design, coniuga la modernità del progetto architettonico per le ampie zone dedicate al relax e all'intrattenimento con un'attenta scelta dei materiali e una cura artigianale dei dettagli. Il risultato è uno spazio multiforme e sorprendente in cui convivono lo scalone di marmo in stile classico, le futuristiche pareti in vetro della discoteca Blue Club e le atmosfere tipicamente inglesi del pub Lord Nelson. Quest'incredibile ricchezza e varietà di stili e di spazi rendono *MSC Lirica* una continua ed entusiasmante scoperta.

Im April 2003 in Neapel vom Stapel gelaufen, gilt *MSC Lirica* als das Schiff, das *MSC Kreuzfahrten* den Ruf des „Erneuerers der Kreuzfahrten" einbrachte. Das avantgardistische Design von De Jorio Design International kombiniert die moderne architektonische Vision aufwändig gestalteter Freizeit- und Entertainmentmöglichkeiten von *MSC Lirica* mit traditionellen Materialien und Handwerkskunst höchster Güte. Das Ergebnis sind auffällige Kontraste, wie z.B. die klassische Prunktreppe aus Marmor, die futuristisch schimmernden Glaswände des Blue Clubs sowie die typisch englische Einrichtung des Lord Nelson-Pubs. Die unglaubliche Bandbreite verschiedener Stile und Annehmlichkeiten macht *MSC Liric*a zu einem Schiff, das man immer wieder neu entdecken kann.

Lancé à Naples en avril 2003, le paquebot *MSC Lirica* impose *MSC Croisières* comme le croisiériste de luxe le plus novateur de ces dernières années. De Jorio Design International y a imaginé des espaces intérieurs d'avant-garde, combinant la modernité des divertissements offerts à bord aux matériaux traditionnels et aux finitions artisanales les plus raffinées. Majestueux escalier de marbre de la réception, parois de verre futuristes et chatoyantes de la discothèque – le Blue Club, décor cossu et confortable d'un pub typiquement britannique – le Lord Nelson : on évolue ici dans un étonnant univers de contrastes. Grâce à son incroyable variété de styles et d'activités, le *MSC Lirica* est un paquebot que l'on ne se lasse jamais d'explorer.

Inaugurado en Nápoles en abril de 2003, *MSC Lirica* fue el barco que consagró a *MSC Cruceros* como la compañía innovadora por excelencia en cruceros de lujo. El precursor diseño de De Jorio Design International aúna una moderna visión arquitectónica en las amplias estancias de ocio y entretenimiento del *MSC Lirica* con los materiales tradicionales y una manufactura artesana de la mejor calidad. Elementos como la grandiosa escalera de mármol clásica, el brillante y futurista cristal de las paredes de la discoteca Blue Club y la decoración típicamente inglesa del pub Lord Nelson ofrecen atractivos contrastes. Precisamente es la increíble variedad de estilos y comodidades lo que hace de *MSC Lirica* un barco que uno nunca se cansa de explorar.

FACTS & FIGURES

Gross Tonnage:	59,058 tons	**Public areas:**	9 lifts, 4 restaurants, 11 bars, casino,
Length:	251.25 metres		Internet café, tennis court, 2 swimming
Height:	54 metres		pools, 2 SPA baths, jogging track, gym,
Width:	28.80 metres		solarium, minigolf, theatre, disco, casino
Cruising speed:	21.7 knots		
Passenger decks:	9		
Cabins:	856 (1.560 passengers, on a double basis/maximum capacity: 2.069)		

Page 197: Detail of the funnel
Page 198/199: Reception

Lord Nelson Pub

Page 202/203: The bridge

Left: The Beverly Hills Bar
Right: Rodeo Drive Shopping area

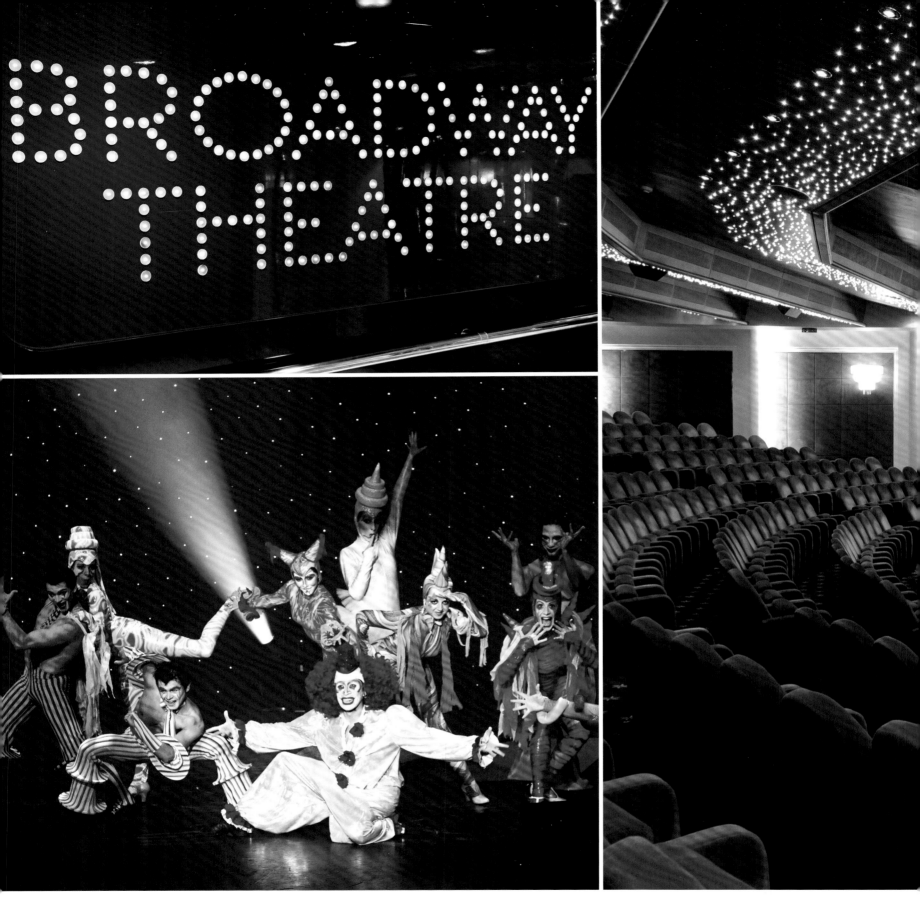

The Broadway Theatre, 713 seats

© 2009 teNeues Verlag GmbH + Co. KG, Kempen

Photo Credits:
© Reto Guntli / zapaimages.com: pp 197–205, 208 top, 208/209, 210–215
© Agi Simoes / zapaimages.com: pp 181–183, 186–189, 191, 193 bottom left, 194/195
© Jörg Tietje / www.joergtietje.com: pp 23–25, 30, 31, 34–47, 52–67, 68/69, 70, 71, 74/75, 80, 81, 88–91, 94–117, 119–123, 126, 127, 131, 132–145, 147–151, 152 top, 152/153, 157 right, 158–160, 162–169, 173 right, 174–179
© Courtesy of MSC Crociere and Ivan Sarfatti / www.ivansarfatti.com: pp 4–21, 26–29, 32/33, 48–51, 68 top, bottom, 72/73, 76 –79, 84–87, 92/93, 124/125, 128–130, 132, 152 bottom, 154–156/157, 161, 170–172, 172/173 middle, 184, 185, 190, 192, 193 top, bottom right, 206/207, 208 bottom, 216/217, cover, back cover

Texts by Michael Benis
Translations by Zoratti studio editoriale:
Chiara Pagnani (Italian)
Anne Zink (German)
Laurence Lenglet (French)
Almudena Sasiain (Spanish)

Design by Silke Braun
Production by Nele Jansen, teNeues Verlag
Color separation by Laudert GmbH + Co. KG, Vreden

Published by teNeues Publishing Group

teNeues Verlag Gmbh + Co. KG
Am Selder 37, 47906 Kempen, Germany
Phone: 0049-2152-916-0
Fax: 0049-2152-916-111
e-mail: books@teneues.de

Press department: Andrea Rehn
Phone: 0049-2152-916-202
e-mail: arehn@teneues.de

teNeues Publishing Company
16 West 22nd Street, New York, NY 10010, USA
Phone: 001-212-627-9090
Fax: 001-212-627-9511

teNeues Publishing UK Ltd.
York Villa, York Road, Byfleet, KT14 7HX, Great Britain
Phone: 0044-1932-4035-09
Fax: 0044-1932-4035-14

teNeues France S.A.R.L.
93, rue Bannier, 45000 Orléans, France
Phone: 0033-2-3854-1071
Fax: 0033-2-3862-5340

www.teneues.com

ISBN 978-3-8327-9310-4

Printed in Italy

Bibliographic information published by the Deutsche Nationalbibliothek.
The Deutsche Nationalbibliothek lists this publication in the Deutsche Nationalbibliografie; detailed bibliographic data are available in the Internet at http://dnb.d-nb.de.